The Finnish Christmas Cookbook

Marit Peters

Contents

Introduction

Christmas is a popular time of the year in Finland and has many of the familiar Christmas traditions of other nations such as trees and decorations, parties, markets and customs. Finland has a great Christmas atmosphere as it is located in northern Europe so has snow, reindeer, trees used for Christmas trees and it is even said that Santa Claus lives in northern Finland.

Finland has many of its own Christmas customs to reflect Finnish culture. It has its own distinctive Christmas food eaten throughout the Christmas season and during the main days of Christmas.

Learn about Christmas in Finland and try some Finnish Christmas foods with this book - The Finnish Christmas Cookbook

Helsinki

Salmon Soup

Ingredients

800g/1.7 lb of diced salmon fillet with no skin
700g/1.5 lb of diced potato
2 sliced leeks
pinch of allspice
3 bay leaves
chopped fresh dill
1.3 litres/2.7 pints of fish stock
340ml of cream
butter
salt
pepper

Put some butter in a saucepan. Cook the leaks in the butter for 5 minutes.

Add the potatoes, cover them with water, bring to the boil and cook for 5 minutes. Add the salmon and bay leaves and cook on a low heat for 5 minutes.

Add the fish stock, cream and some salt, pepper and allspice. Cook on a low heat for 16 minutes.

Add some dill when serving.

Finnish Mustard

Ingredients

30g/1 oz of mustard powder
2 tablespoons of apple cider vinegar
135g/4.7 oz of caster sugar
240ml/8.11 oz of single cream
1 tablespoon of vegetable oil
1 tablespoon of lemon juice

Mix the vinegar and mustard.

Put the vinegar ans mustard mix in a pan with the rest of the ingredients. Boil then cook on a medium hear for 10 minutes stirring frequently until the sauce thickens.

Cool then store in sterilised jars or containers.

Carrot Casserole

Ingredients

230g/8.11 oz of cooked rice
4 grated carrot
2 eggs
20g/1 third of a cup of dry breadcrumbs
2 teaspoons of sugar
3 tablespoons of melted butter
butter
500ml/2 cups of milk
salt

Mix the milk, rice. sugar, eggs, carrot and some salt in a bowl. Grease a baking dish with some butter and pour in the rice mix.

Mix the melted butter with the breadcrumbs. Put on top of the rice mix. Cook in a preheated oven at 190C/375F for 45 minutes - until browned.

Dill Sauce

Ingredients

240ml/1 cup of buttermilk
2 tablespoons of lemon juice
half a finely chopped onion
1 tablespoon of finely chopped dill

Mix the ingredients in a bowl.

Refrigerate for 2 hours.

Liver Pate

Ingredients

700g/1 and a half lb of pork liver
200g/ half a lb of pork fat
2 chopped onions
half a teaspoon of ground allspice
1 teaspoon of white pepper
1 and a half tablespoons of salt
1 tablespoon of sugar
1 teaspoon of dried marjoram
2 eggs
125g/4oz of wheat flour
700ml/3 cups of milk
100g/3.5 oz of margarine

Blend the liver, pork fat, onions, marjoram, allspice, pepper and salt together. Mix the egg with the flour and milk and add to the other ingredients. Melt the margarine and add this to the mixture.

Place the mixture in tins. Put the tins in a baking dish and pour hot water until the water is half way up the level of the tins. Cover with foil and cook for 1 hour at 175C/347F.

Cool before serving.

Mushroom Salad

Ingredients

570g/1 lb 4 oz of sliced mushrooms
2 tablespoons of finely chopped chives
60ml/2 fl oz of cream
1 tablespoon of red wine vinegar
pinch of salt
pinch of sugar
pinch of pepper

Boil a little water and salt in a pan. Add the mushrooms, boil then cover and cook on a low heat for 1 minute.

Drain the mushrooms and leave to cool.

Mix the chives, cream, vinegar and some salt, sugar and pepper with the mushrooms. Mix and put in the refrigerator for 1 hour.

Cranberry Sauce

Ingredients

450g/1 lb of cranberries
120ml/half a cup of water
560g/1 and a quarter lb of sugar

Add the water, sugar and the cranberries to a pan. Bring to the boil then and cook on a low heat for 15 minutes until the berries have broken up.

Ground Meat Soup

Ingredients

700g/1.5 lb of minced/ground beef
2 chopped onions
4 peeled and chopped carrots
1 chopped stick of celery
200g/7 oz of peeled chopped swede/rutabaga
1 kg/2.2 lb of peeled and chopped potatoes
fresh dill
2 litres/2.11 pints of beef stock/broth

Put the stock in a pan and boil.

Add the rutabaga, carrot, celery, onion and potatoes. Cover and cook on a low heat for 10 minutes.

Put the beef in another pan with some oil and cook for 6 minutes.

Add to the vegetable mix in the other pan. Cook for 5 minutes - until everything is cooked.

Add some dill before serving.

Beetroot Salad

Ingredients

4 beetroot
3 carrots
3 potatoes
1 finely chopped onion
2 peeled and chopped green apples
1 chopped gherkin
salt
pepper

dressing

180ml/6.3 fl oz of whipped cream
2 teaspoons of lemon juice
pinch of sugar
pinch of salt
pinch of pepper

Put the beetroot in a pan of hot water. Bring to the boil then simmer for 20 minutes - until cooked.

Leave to cool then peel and chop. Keep a little bit of the liquid.

Put the potatoes in a pan of water. Add a little salt. Bring to the boil then cook on a medium heat for 20 minutes - until cooked.

Leave to cool then peel and chop.

Put the carrots in a pan of boiling water. Add the carrots and boil for 10 minutes until cooked. Peel and chop.

Put the ingredients in a bowl in layers. Put some salt on each layer and begin and end with a layer of beetroot. Mix the ingredients when serving.

For the dressing, mix the ingredients with a tablespoon of the beetroot cooking liquid. Serve with the salad.

Split Pea Soup

Ingredients

770g/1.7 lb of split peas
270g/9.5 oz of cooked chopped ham
400g/14 oz of chopped potatoes
120g/4.2 oz of chopped carrots
half a chopped onion
4 allspice berries
1.2 litres5 cups of water
salt
pepper

Put the water, split peas, ham and allspice berries in a pan. Cover and cook on a low heat for 1 hour.

Put the carrots, onion, potato and some salt and pepper in the pan and boil then cover and cook on a low heat for 35 minutes.

Remove the allspice berries before serving.

Finnish Christmas Facts

The traditional Christmas dinner starts with fish. The dishes include herrings in different sauces, gravlax salmon, roe and smoked fish. Lutefix is sometimes served. Boiled potatoes is a common vegetable served with the fish.

The main course includes Finnish casseroles such as liver, potato, carrot and rutabaga. A Christmas ham is popular as the main dish along with a beetroot salad and a variety of other salads. Although the main meat course for Finnish Christmas dinner is traditionally a ham, other dishes such as turkey are served in some households.

The last course is the sweet course with plum pastries, gingerbread and other cookies and a variety of cakes.

In Finland rice porridge is served for breakfast on Christmas Eve.

Mulled wine - Glögg in Finnish - is a popular Christmas drink in Finland. There are many recipes and alcoholic and non-alcoholic versions.

Finnish people have small Christmas parties - pikkujoulut - at workplaces, schools, clubs and among friends during the Christmas period.

Beetroot Salad

Liver Casserole

Vegetable and Barley Salad

Ingredients

150g/5.3 oz of chopped swede/rutabaga
150g/5.3 oz of chopped carrot
150g/5.3 oz of chopped parsnip
110g/3.8 oz of feta cheese
150g/5.3 oz of barley
1 chopped lettuce
2 tablespoons of chopped walnuts
120g/4.2 oz of destoned chopped prunes
chopped fresh parsley
100ml/3.3 fl oz of yogurt
1 teaspoon of honey
salt
pepper
oil

Put the swede, parsnip and carrot on a baking tray. Add some oil and bake in a preheated oven at 210C/410F for 25 minutes.

Put the barley in a pan of hot water. Boil then cook on a low heat for 35 minutes - until cooked.

Mix the yogurt, olive oil, honey and lemon juice in a bowl. Add the barley, parsnip, carrot and swede and mix. Add the parsley and lettuce. Top with the crumbled feta cheese.

Pea Sauce

Ingredients

500g/17 oz of green peas
1 tablespoon of flour
2 teaspoons of sugar
1 tablespoon of butter
40ml/1.4 fl oz of cream
salt

Put 240ml/1 cup of water in a pan with a pinch of salt. Mix in the flour. Boil then cook on a low heat for 5 minutes.

Add the peas and a little more salt and the sugar. Simmer for 5 minutes.

Add the cream and bring to the boil. Stir in the butter before serving.

Cucumber Salad

Ingredients

2 sliced cucumbers
120ml/half a cup of sour cream
2 tablespoons of white vinegar
2 tablespoons of white sugar
1 teaspoon of dried dill
1 teaspoon of dried parsley
1 teaspoon of salt

Put the cucumber on a plate. Add some salt and leave for 20 minutes. Use a paper towel to get rid of excess moisture from the cucumber.

Mix the sour cream, vinegar, dill, sugar and parsley in a bowl. Add the cucumber to the bowl.

Place in the refrigerator for 10 hours.

Potato Casserole

Ingredients

1 kg/2.2 lb of potatoes
55g/1.9 oz of flour
550ml/2 and 1 third cups of warm milk
55g/1.9 oz of melted butter
1 teaspoon of salt
pinch of allspice
2 tablespoons of syrup

Put the potatoes in a pan of water and boil. Cover then cook on a medium heat for 20 minutes - until the potatoes are cooked.

Drain the potatoes. Take off the skins and mash in a bowl. Stir in the flour then leave for 3 hours.

Add the butter, milk salt and some allspice. Mix. Add some of the syrup and mix.

Put the mix in a greased baking dish. Put the rest of the syrup on top. Cook in a preheated oven at 160C/320F for 2 and a half hours.

Green Bean Salad

Ingredients

450g/1 lb of chopped green beans
3 peeled and chopped tomatoes
half a sliced onion
2 tablespoons of chopped dill
1 teaspoon of sugar
1 tablespoon of lemon juice
250ml/8 fl oz of sour cream
salt
pepper

Put the green beans in a pan and cover with water. Add a little salt and boil for 12 minutes - until cooked. Drain them and leave to cool.

Put the green beans, sour cream, dill, sugar, lemon , some salt and pepper, tomatoes and onion in a bowl. Mix.

Spinach Soup

Ingredients

1 kg/2.1 lb of spinach
2 litres/4.2 pints of chicken (or vegetable) stock/broth
3 tablespoons of butter
2 tablespoons of flour
salt
pepper
pinch of nutmeg

Put the chicken stock in a pan and bring to the boil. Add the spinach and cook on a low heat for 8 minutes.

Pour the soup through a sieve into a bowl. Reserve the liquid and finely chop the spinach.

Put the butter in a pan and melt then stir in the flour to make a paste. Add the chicken stock/broth and whisk. Boil, then add some salt and pepper and cook on a low heat for 6 minutes.

Red Cabbage With Apple

Ingredients

1 chopped red cabbage
1 chopped green apples
1 chopped onion
55g/1.9 oz of brown sugar
2 tablespoons of butter
2 teaspoons of sea salt
pinch of allspice
pinch of nutmeg
2 tablespoons of lingonberry or redcurrant jam/jelly
2 tablespoons of apple cider vinegar
pepper

Fry the onions and apples in the butter in a pan for 5 minutes.

Add the cabbage and cook for 7 minutes.

Add the sugar, vinegar, allspice, nutmeg and sea salt. Cover and cook in a low heat for 10 minutes.

Add the jam, take off the cover and cook for 6 minutes on a low heat. Season with some pepper.

Rutabaga Casserole

Ingredients

830g/1.8 lb of peeled swede/rutabaga cut into pieces
1 egg
pinch of nutmeg
pinch of dry ginger
1 tablespoon of syrup
55g/2 oz of dry breadcrumbs
145ml/5 fl oz of cream
butter
salt
pepper

Put the rutabaga in a pan with some cold water, some butter and some salt. Boil then cook on a low heat for 15 minutes - until cooked. Drain and mash.

Mix the rutabaga with the cream, egg, ginger, nutmeg, syrup, half the breadcrumbs and some salt and pepper. Put the mix in a baking dish. top with the rest of the breadbrumbs and some pieces of butter. Cook in a preheated oven at 160C/320F for 1 hour.

Salmon with Sour Cream

Ingredients

1 salmon fillet
1 teaspoon of salt
1 teaspoon of lemon juice
2 tablespoons of lemon juice
black pepper
fresh dill
430ml/14 fl oz of sour cream

Put the salmon fillet in a baking dish. Season with salt and pepper and add the lemon juice. Mix the sour cream, lemon zest and some black pepper.

Put the sour cream mix on top of the salmon. Cook in a preheated oven at 175C/350F for 25 minutes.

Roe with Eggs

Ingredients

boiled eggs halved with yolk removed
fish roe
sour cream
dill

Put fish roe on top of the boiled egg halves. Top with sour cream and dill.

Finnish Christmas Facts

A survey of the Finnish Christmas dinner found that 82% of houses had a Christmas ham. 64% had gravlax, 77% had rutabaga casserole, 77% had carrot casserole, 76% had plum Christmas Tarts. 40% of people prefer the traditional Christmas dishes and 48% like to try some different dishes.

Lutefisk is a popular in western Finland. Lutefix is a Scandinavian delicacy. It consists of dried whitefish, such as cod, which had been soaked in lye. It takes on a jelly like texture and is inedible during this stage in the cooking process. To become ready for eating the fish is soaked for several days in water which is changed daily. The fish is then boiled and steamed and served with boiled potatoes and white sauce.

Game meat is popular for Christmas in Lapland.

Shellfish and roe are popular Christmas dinner dishes in southern Finland.

Karelian hot pot is especially popular in eastern Finland.

Beetroot salad - Rosolli - was first eaten at Christmas by rich families in south west Finland in the 1700s.

Herring Salad

Ingredients

530g/1.2 lb of chopped marinated herring fillets
530g/1.2 lb of chopped boiled potatoes
200g/7 oz of chopped pickles
half a finely sliced red onion
2 tablespoons of chopped dill
1 tablespoon of spirit/white vinegar
210g/7.4 oz of sour cream
salt
pepper

Mix the herring, potatoes, onion and pickles in a bowl.

In another bowl mix the dill, sour cream, vinegar and some salt and pepper.

Combine the two mixes. Refrigerate for 1 hour.

Serve on buttered rye bread or as a side dish.

Jansson's Temptation

Fried Herring

Fish in Jelly

Ingredients

900g/2 lb of chopped skinned white fish
sliced hard boiled egg
sliced tomato

jelly

2 tablespoons (7 sheets) of gelatine
470ml/1 pint of fish stock
2 egg whites
salt
pepper

cooking stock

4 allspice berries
1 bay leaf
4 peppercorns
1 tablespoon of spirit/white vinegar

Put the cooking stock ingredients in a pan with 1 litre/1 quart of water. Boil for 15 minutes.

Add the fish and boil for 10 minutes - until cooked. Drain and keep the fish and stock.

Mix the gelatine with a little water. Put in a pan with the

egg whites and the fish stock. Boil, then leave for 16 minutes. Strain the liquid. Add some salt and pepper and leave to cool.

Take a jelly/jello mould and put eggs and tomato pieces in it. Add some of the stock and refrigerate until the jelly sets.

Add the fish, pour over the stock and refrigerate until the jelly has set. Remove the jelly from the mould whole to serve.

Gravad Lax

Ingredients

2 sides of salmon with skin on
2 large bunches of fresh dill
125g/4 oz of sea salt
250g/8 oz of sugar
30g/1 oz black pepper (preferably freshly ground)

Chop up the dill and add to the salt, pepper and sugar. Mix.

Put a third of the mix on some clingfilm/plastic wrap. Put a salmon fillet on the mix skin side down. Put another third of the mix on top. Put the other salmon fillet on top with the skin on top. Add the rest of the mix.

Wrap the fish in the clingfilm. Put in a dish a put another flat object such as a plate on top. Put a weight on top such as a brick. Place in the refrigerator for 3 days turning the fish over about 5 times.

Remove the dill mix before serving the salmon sliced.

Jansson's Temptation

Ingredients

10 peeled and chopped potatoes
1 sliced onion
18 sprat fillets (in brine or Swedish ansjovis)
dried breadcrumbs
butter
160ml/5.4 fl oz of cream
160ml/5.4 fl oz of milk
salt
pepper

Cook the onion in some butter in a pan for 5 minutes. Add the potatoes and cook for 4 minutes.

Put half the potato and onion mix in a baking dish. Put half the sprats on top. Put the rest of the potato and onion mix on top followed by the rest of the sprats. Pour the milk and cream over the top and sprinkle on the breadcrumbs.

Cook in a preheated oven at 200C/400F for 50 minutes - until the potatoes are cooked.

An alternative is *Ham Temptation* where the sprats are replaced by pieces of ham.

Salted Salmon

Ingredients

1 salmon fillet
2 tablespoons of salt
2 teaspoons of sugar

Rub the salt and sugar on the salmon. Put the salmon in a glass bowl and cover with a glass lid.

Leave for 4 days in the refrigerator.

Slice thinly to serve.

Fried Herring

Ingredients

herring fillets
flour
beaten egg
breadcrumbs
lime zest
salt
pepper

Mix some flour with some salt and pepper.

Coat the fish in the flour.

Then coat the fish in the egg.

Finish by coating the fish in breadcrumbs and a little lime zest.

Heat some oil and butter in a frying pan. Cook the fish over a medium heat for 3 minutes on each side.

Roast Pork

Ingredients

453g/1 lb of pork belly
1 tablespoon of sea salt
1 teaspoon of chopped sage
1 teaspoon of black pepper
1 tablespoon of chopped thyme
chopped dill

Mix the sea salt, thyme, sage and pepper in a bowl. Rub this mix over the pork. Roll the pork up and secure with twine. Put in a baking dish and refrigerate for 10 hours.

Put some foil over the pork and cook in a preheated oven at 176C/350F for 2 hours. Then remove the foil and cook at 148C/300F for 2 hours - until the pork is cooked. Leave to cool and keep the cooking juices.

Remove the twine from the pork. Cut into slices. Put some of the cooking juices in a pan and fry the pork until crisp on all sides.

Sprinkle some dill and parsley on top.

Finnish Christmas Facts

Christmas ham is the most popular meat for Christmas dinner. It became popular during the 20th century. Previously a selection of different meats were served; lamb was common.

Rice porridge became more widely eaten in the late 1800s as rice became more available, Before then porridge at Christmas was made out of barley, oats and rye.

It is said that the traditional Finnish Christmas dinner is simple with just a few ingredients.

Christmas bread - joululimppu - is always served at the Christmas dinner table. This is a loaf which has both savory and sweet spices.

The Christmas ham served at Finnish Christmas dinner is often served with peas, plums and Finnish mustard.

Finnish casseroles are served at the Finnish Christmas dinner. These are normally carrot (porkkanalaatikko), potato (perunalaatikko) rutabaga (lanttulaatikko) and liver casserole (maksalaatikko).

Two traditional Finish Christmas cookies are gingerbread (pipari) and plum pastries (joulutorttu).

Karelian Hot Pot

Ingredients

425g/15 oz of cubed pork
425g/15 oz of cubed beef
2 sliced onions
2 chopped carrots
1 tablespoon of black peppercorns
1 teaspoon of allspice berries
salt
pepper
oil

Cook the beef and pork for 6 minutes in some hot oil in a pan to brown.

Put a layer of the meat in a casserole dish dish. Add a layer of the carrots and onions. Add some black peppercorns, allspice berries and some salt and pepper. Repeat the layers until the ingredients are used up. Add cold water to cover the items in the dish.

Put in a preheated oven at 150C/302F for 3 hours - until the meat is cooked.

Baked Ham

Ingredients

1 salted/brined boneless gammon/ham
4 tablespoons of honey
110g/4.8 oz of Finnish sweet mustard
dry breadcrumbs

Rinse the ham.

Cut slices in the top of the ham. Put on a baking tray and cook in a preheated oven at 125C/257F until done. Cooking time is 50 minute per 1 kg/2/2 lb.

Remove the skin and fat from the ham.

Mix the honey and mustard. Paste over the ham. Sprinkle on the breadcrumbs and push them into the mustard. Cook for 12 minutes in the oven - until the top has browned.

Roast Turkey

Ingredients

1 turkey
2 halved onions
2 chopped carrots
1 orange cut into 4 pieces
1 tablespoon of dried cranberries
1 teaspoon of juniper berries
parsley
butter
salt
pepper

Rub the turkey with butter and sprinkle salt and pepper on top. Put half the onion in the turkey cavity with the orange pieces, juniper berries and cranberries.

Put the other onion and carrots in a baking dish. Put the turkey on top. Cover with foil. Cook in a preheated oven at 180C for 40 minutes per kg/2.2 lb for the first 4 kg/8.8lb of the turkey weight, then 45 minutes for each additional 1 kg/2.2 lb.

40 minutes before the end of cooking remove the foil and baste regularly.

Liver Casserole

Ingredients

310g/11 oz of minced/ground liver
180g/6.3 oz of rice
2 chopped onions
110g/3.8 oz of raisins
1 teaspoon of marjoram
1 egg
butter
4 tablespoons of syrup
1.1 litres/4 and a half cups of milk
100ml/3.3 fl oz of water
2 teaspoons of salt
pepper

Put the rice in a pan with the milk and water. Bring to a boil then cover and cook on a low heat for about 10 minutes until the rice is cooked.

Fry the onions in some butter for 6 minutes.

Mix the rice, liver, onions, egg, marjoram, raisins, some salt and pepper and syrup in a bowl. Put in a baking dish. Put some pieces of butter on top.

Cook in a preheated casserole at 180C/356F for 1 and a half hours.

Serve with redcurrant or lingonberry jam.

Christmas Ham

Ginger Cookies

Pork with Horseradish

Ingredients

900g/2 lb pork cut into cubes
1 chopped onion
1 chopped carrot
1 chopped stick of celery
60ml/a quarter of a cup of horseradish sauce
475ml/2 cups of water
240ml/1 cup of vinegar
2 tablespoons of butter
1 teaspoon of caraway seeds
half a teaspoon of pepper
1 tablespoon of salt

Cook the pork in the butter until it is browned.

Add the onion, celery, carrot, water, vinegar, caraway seeds and salt and pepper. Cover and cook on a low heat for 2 hours.

Put the pork on a plate.

Puree the cooking liquid in a blender (or push it through a sieve). Pour the liquid over the pork and put the horseradish sauce on top.

Meatballs

Ingredients

453g/1 lb of minced/ground beef
150g/1 cup of dry breadcrumbs
1 finely chopped onion
1 egg
2 tablespoons of flour
240ml/1 cup of double/whipping cream
250ml of milk
salt
pepper
1 teaspoon of allspice

Mix the breadcrumbs, beef, onion, half the cream, egg allspice and some salt and pepper in a bowl. Make into balls.

Cook in butter for 7 minutes on all sides of the balls to brown them.

Reserve the juices in the pan and put the meatballs on a plate.

Put the flour in the pan and mix with the pan juices and cook for 2 minutes to make a paste. Add the rest of the cream and milk and heat whisking all the time.

Put the meatballs back in the pan and cook on a low heat

for 20 minutes.

Finnish Christmas Facts

The Finnish word for Christmas is joulu.

The main day in the Finnish Christmas is December 24th.

Christmas in Finland ends on St Knut's Day - January 13th.

It is traditional to have a sauna on Christmas Eve in Finland.

Christmas markets are held from November in Finland with foods, drinks and crafts.

In the capital Helsinki opening of Christmas is celebrated with the lighting of the Christmas lights on Aleksanterinkatu.

The oldest and largest Christmas market in Finland is the one in Senate Square market called Tuomaan markkinat.

Finland has a tradition of Christmas peace where war is put on hold. At noon on December 24th peace is proclaimed in a televised ceremony from Brinkkala Hall balcony near Turku Cathedral in Turku, Finland's oldest city.

A popular Christmas song in Finland is Lasten Meelise, which means The Children's Joy.

Roast Beef With Juniper

Ingredients

1 rump/sirloin beef joint
1 sliced onion
14 juniper berries
1 teaspoon of lemon zest
2 tablespoons of fresh thyme
1 teaspoon of black pepper corns
thyme sprigs
oil
sea salt

Mix the juniper berries, peppercorns, thyme, lemon juice, some oil and some sea salt to make a paste. Rub over the beef.

Put the onion and thyme sprigs in a baking dish. Put the beef on top. Leave for 2 hours.

Cook the beef in a preheated oven at 220C/428F for 30 minutes. Cook at 180C/356F for 45 minutes. This will be cooked for medium rare. Cook for another 10 minutes for medium.

Almond Cookies

Ingredients

85g/3 oz of ground almonds
finely chopped almonds
egg white
340g/12 oz of flour
65g/3 oz of sugar
255g/9 oz butter
extra sugar

Put the flour, 85/3 oz of sugar and ground almonds in a bowl. Add the butter and make a dough. Make into finger shapes. Dip the cookies in some egg white then dip in the extra sugar and almonds.

Put in a greased baking tray and cook in a preheated oven at 204C/400F for 13 minutes - until cooked.

Christmas Tarts

Ingredients

dough

250g/8.8 oz of cold butter cubes
330g/11.6 oz of flour
6 teaspoons of sugar
140ml/4.7 oz of cold water
salt
plum jam
powdered/confectioners' sugar

For the dough, mix the flour sugar and some salt. Add the butter. Add the water and make a dough. Roll out the dough. Divide into two and wrap both pieces in plastic wrap/clingfilm and refrigerate for 40 minutes.

Roll out the dough pieces and cut each piece into about 7 squares. Put plum jam in the middle of a square. Make a cut from each corner to the centre. Fold the corners of each of the four triangle shapes over the jam. Repeat with the rest of the dough squares.

Put on a baking tray lined with parchment/greaseproof paper and cook in a preheated oven at 220C/440F for 15 minutes.

Dust with powdered sugar.

Finnish Christmas Food Facts

Santa Claus - Joulupukki in Finnish - gives gifts to children on December 24th, Christmas Eve. It is believed that Santa lives in Lapland in northern Finland. People from around the world sent letters to Santa in Finland. A theme park called Santa Claus Village is located in Rovaniemi in Lapland.

On December 24th a television show called The Santa Claus Hotline is broadcast from Rovaniemi where children can talk to Santa.

Children write letters to Santa which are left in mailboxes or glass jars to be collected by Santa's Elves.

In Finnish Merry Christmas is 'Hyvää joulua'.

St Lucia's Day is celebrated on the 13th December - especially among Swedish speaking Finns.

On the 13th December a chosen girl with candles in her hair and dressed in white tours places that need light such as hospitals and retirement homes. There is also a parade in Helsinki

Prune Soup

Ingredients

230g/8.11 oz of prunes
1 litre/4 cups of water
150g/3 quarters of a cup of sugar
3 tablespoons of cornflour/cornstarch
pinch of cinnamon

Put the water, prunes, sugar and some cinnamon in a pan and boil for 16 minutes. Cool.

Put cornflour in a bowl with a little water and make a smooth mix. Add to the prune mix and bring to the boil, stirring all the time,

Serve with rice pudding.

Rice Pudding

Ingredients

220g/1 cup of rice
55g/2 oz of sliced unblanched almonds
720ml/3 cups of milk
56g/2 oz of melted butter
90g/3.17 oz of sugar
3 beaten eggs
cinnamon
salt

Put the rice in a saucepan. Add double the amount of water to rice and bring to a boil. Cover and cook on a low heat for 20 minutes -until cooked.

Rinse the rice. Mix with the eggs, milk, sugar and some salt.

Put the rice in a greased baking dish. Sprinkle the almonds and some cinnamon over the top.

Cook in a preheated oven at 176C/350F for 1 hour.

Put a whole almond somewhere in the pudding.

Christmas Almonds

Ingredients

350g/12 oz of almonds
2 and a half tablespoons of honey
2 tablespoons of water
1 tablespoon of oil
5 tablespoons of sugar
1 tablespoon of cinnamon
2 teaspoons of salt

Put the almonds in a baking tray lined with greaseproof/parchment paper. Put in a preheated oven at 230C/446F and cook for 12 minutes.

Put the honey, oil and water in a pan. Boil. Add the almonds to the pan. Boil stirring all the time until most of the liquid has gone.

Put the sugar, salt and cinnamon on a plate and mix. Coat the almonds in the mix.

Christmas Bread

Ingredients

dough

250g/8.8 oz of flour
2 teaspoons of yeast
1 teaspoon of salt
1 teaspoon of cumin
2 fl oz of warm water
1 tablespoons of butter

95g/3.3 oz of rye flour
175ml/6 fl oz of hot water

Put the hot water and rye in a bowl and leave for 4 hours.

For the dough mix all the ingredients and the rye mix. Make a dough and knead for 20 minutes. Make into a ball. Put in a bowl and cover with a damp towel. Leave for 95 minutes.

Put the dough on a baking tray lined with parchment paper and cook in a preheated oven at 200C/400F for 40 minutes until cooked.

Jelly Candies

Ingredients

6 teaspoons of pectin
481g/17 oz of blackberries
113g/4 oz of golden/corn syrup
1 tablespoon of lemon juice
481g/17 oz of sugar

vanilla sugar

453g/16 oz of sugar mixed with a drop of vanilla essence

Blend the blackberries to make a smooth mix. Strain into a bowl.

Spray a cake pan with vegetable oil. Add some parchment/baking paper to the pan and spray with more oil.

Mix 85g/3 oz of sugar with the pectin.

Put the blackberry mix into a pan and boil. Add the sugar and pectin mix and boil. Add the syrup and the rest of the sugar. Boil for 10 minutes stirring all the time.

Take off the heat and add the lemon juice. Pour the mix into the cake tray. Leave to cool for 8 hours.

Cut the blackberry jelly into squares. Coat with the vanilla sugar.

Runeberg Tortes

Christmas Tarts

Ginger Cookies

Ingredients

368g/13 oz of butter
210g/7.4 oz of sugar
280g/9.8 oz of syrup
4 teaspoons of cinnamon
3 teaspoons of ginger
1 teaspoon of allspice
1 tablespoon of lemon zest
2 eggs
610g/1.3 lb of flour
2 teaspoons of baking soda

Put the sugar, syrup, butter, ginger, cinnamon and allspice in a pan. Heat stirring all the time until the pan nearly boils.

Put the mix in a bowl and allow to cool.

Add the eggs, flour and baking soda to the mix and stir to make a dough.

Put the dough in the refrigerator for 8 hours.

Roll out the dough and cut into shapes.

Put on a baking sheet and cook in a preheated oven at 176C/350F for 15 minutes.

Oven Pancake

Ingredients

2 eggs
500ml/2 cups of milk
2 tablespoons of lemon juice
1 teaspoon of lemon zest
2 tablespoons of sugar
half a teaspoon of cardamom mixed with some sugar
120g/1 cup of flour
55g/2 oz of butter
salt

Put the eggs in a bowl with the milk, sugar, lemon juice, lemon zest and a pinch of salt. Whisk together. Add the flour and make a batter.

Put the butter in a baking dish. Put in a preheated oven at 225C/437F until the butter has melted. Coat the pan with the butter. Pour in the batter and cook for 30 minutes.

Sprinkle the cardamom and sugar mix over the top.

Cardamom Buns

Ingredients

1 kg/2.2 lb of flour
175g/6.1 oz of butter
1 egg
50g/1.7 oz of yeast
198g/7 oz of sugar
250g/8.8 oz of flour
500ml/1 pint of warm milk
1 teaspoon of sea salt
1 teaspoon of cardamom

wash made up of one beaten egg, 1 tablespoon of water and a pinch of sugar

Mix the milk and yeast. Add the egg, sugar, cardamom and salt. Add the flour and make a dough. Add the butter and knead for 10 minutes.

Put the dough in a bowl and cover with a tea/kitchen towel. Leave in a warm place for 1 hour.

Make into 16 buns. Put on baking sheets lined with parchment/greaseproof paper. Cover with a tea/kitchen towel and leave for 30 minutes.

Brush with the wash. Bake in a preheated oven at 225C/435F for 15 minutes.

Runeberg Tortes

Ingredients

60g/half a cup of flour
75g/half a cup of ginger cookie crumbs
1 teaspoon o baking powder
7 tablespoons of ground almonds/almond flour
115g/half a cup of butter
9 tablespoons of sugar
3 tablespoons of cream
3 tablespoons of raspberry jelly/jam

icing

6 tablespoons of icing sugar
1 tablespoon of egg white

Mix the crushed ginger cookies, baking powder and almond flour in a bowl.

Mix the butter and sugar in a bowl and make a paste. Add the eggs and mix. Add the cookie and almond flour mix and the flour. Add the cream and make a smooth mixture.

Put the mix into deep muffin tins. Traditionally the cakes are baked in tins 5 cm/2 inches in diameter and 6 cm/2.3 inches high.

Put a hole in the top of each cake and add some jam.

Cook in a preheated oven at 200C/400F for 20 minutes. Leave to cool.

Mix the icing sugar and egg white to make the icing. Put on top of the cake around the jam.

Finnish Christmas Facts

One Finnish Christmas ornament is a small one called himmeli made from straw; it is hung in a window or from the tree.

Finns have a piece of wood shaped like an upside down v with seven electric candles in windows during the Christmas period.

Mistletoe is considered good luck and is often on Christmas trees in Finland.

In Finland, Christmas Eve on December 24th, Christmas Day on December 25th and St. Stephen's Day on December 26th are national holidays.

Hyacinth and poinsettia are popular Christmas flowers.

On Christmas Day Finns normally visit friends and relatives and relax.

During December restaurants in Finland serve a lunch buffet consisting of traditional Finnish foods.

Kissel

Ingredients

270g/9.5 oz of destoned prunes
1.2 litres/5 cups of water
1 stick of cinnamon
110g/3.8 oz of sugar
3 tablespoons of potato flour
1 tablespoon of lemon juice

Put the prunes and cinnamon in a pan with the water bring to the boil and boil fo16 minutes.

Mix the potato flour with a little water and add to the pan stirring all the time.

Cool then remove the cinnamon stick. Add the lemon juice before serving.

Spice Cake

Ingredients

2 eggs
410g/14 oz of sugar
480ml/2 cups of sour cream
2 drops of almond essence
1 teaspoon of cardamom powder
half a teaspoon of cinnamon
half a teaspoon of allspice
1 teaspoon of baking powder
pinch of salt
330g/12 oz of flour
butter
powdered sugar

Mix the sugar, eggs, almond essence, cinnamon, cardamom and sour cream in a bowl. Add the flour, baking soda and a pinch of salt.

Grease a bundt cake pan with some butter. Put the cake mix in the pan.

Put in a preheated oven at 176C/350F for 1 hour 10 minutes - until baked.

Dust the cake with some powdered sugar.

Archipelago Bread

Ingredients

300g/11 oz of flour
60g/2.11 oz or rye flour
75g/2.6 oz of bran
90g/3.2 oz of malt flour
370ml of buttermilk or sour milk
75g/2.6 oz of black treacle/dark syrup
3 tablespoons of oil
3 teaspoons of yeast
1 teaspoon of salt
butter

Warm the milk and put in a bowl. Add the yeast, malt flour, bran syrup and salt. Mix in the rye flour. Mix in the flour and oil and make a dough.

Divide the dough into two pieces and put into two bread tins which have been greased with butter. Cover the tins with damp tea/dish towels. Leave for 1 hour.

Put the bread in a the middle of a preheated oven at 175C/350F and cook for 1 hour. Brush the bread with a little syrup and cook at 140C/284F for 25 minutes.

Christmas Hot Chocolate

Ingredients

1 litre/2.11 pints of milk
5 tablespoons of cocoa powder
1 teaspoon of dried cardamom
pinch of nutmeg
3 tablespoons of sugar
1 tablespoon of grated chocolate

Heat the milk in a pan. Add the cocoa powder, grated chocolate, sugar, nutmeg and cardamom. Bring to a boil whisking all the time.

Wine Glögi

Ingredients

750ml/1.6 pints of dry red wine
750ml/1.6 pints of port wine
354ml/1 and a half cups of brandy
peel of 1 orange
85g/two thirds of cup of sugar
2 cinnamon sticks
1 tablespoon cardamom Seeds
12 cloves
128g/1 cup raisins
128g/1 cup almonds

Put all the ingredients in a saucepan. Simmer for 25 minutes stirring several times. Do not boil.

Serve warm.

Apple Glögi

Ingredients

1.3 litres/5 and a half cups of apple juice
1 teaspoon of cloves
1 teaspoon of cardamom seeds
1 stick of cinnamon
1 teaspoon of grated fresh ginger

Put the ingredients in a pan. Cook on a low heat for 30 minutes. Strain before serving.

Photo Credits

Helsinki

https://commons.wikimedia.org/wiki/File:Senate_Square_at_Christmas_time_-_Marit_Henriksson_3.jpg

Marit Henriksson

22 December 2018

Prune Tarts

https://commons.wikimedia.org/wiki/File:Joulutorttuja.jpg

Mysid

24 December 2006

Christmas Ham

https://commons.wikimedia.org/wiki/File:Christmas_ham.jpg

Santeri Viinamäki

4 December 2016

Gingerbread

https://commons.wikimedia.org/wiki/File:Freshly_bake
d_gingerbread_-_Christmas_2004.jpg

Jonik

25 December 2004

Front Cover

https://commons.wikimedia.org/wiki/File:Stamp_of_Finl
and_-_1990_-_Colnect_47322_-
_Santa_Claus_reindeer.jpegstamp

Post of Finland

1990

Liver Casserole

https://commons.wikimedia.org/wiki/File:Finnish_maks
alaatikko.JPG

PtG

3 August 2012

Jansson's Temptation

https://commons.wikimedia.org/wiki/File:Janssons_frest
else_close-up.jpg

erik forsberg

24 December 2010

Runeborg Tortes

https://commons.wikimedia.org/wiki/File:Runeberg%27s_tortes.jpg

k

1 February 2022

Beetroot Salad

https://commons.wikimedia.org/wiki/File:Rosolli.jpg

Miia Ranta

20 July 2011

Fried Herring

https://commons.wikimedia.org/wiki/File:FriedHerring.jpg

Jgu

15 February 2010

www.ingramcontent.com/pod-product-compliance
Lightning Source LLC
Chambersburg PA
CBHW060452160726

47992CB00003B/1187